# Things You Can Do While You're NAKED

Jaime Andrews
Jessica Doherty

SANTA MONICA PRESS

Published by: Santa Monica Press LLC
P.O. Box 1076
Santa Monica, CA 90406-1076
1-800-784-9553
www.santamonicapress.com
books@santamonicapress.com

Printed in the United States

Santa Monica Press books are available at special quantity discounts when purchased in bulk by corporations, organizations, or groups. Please call our Special Sales department at 1-800-784-9553.

ISBN 1-59580-016-6

Library of Congress Cataloging-in-Publication Data

Andrews, Jaime, 1977-
 Things you can do while you're naked / by Jaime Andrews and Jessica Doherty.
    p. cm.
 ISBN 1-59580-016-6
 1.  Nudity--Humor. 2.  Conduct of life--Humor.  I. Doherty, Jessica, 1977- II. Title.

PN6231.N9A53 2006
818'.602--dc22

To our parents for laughing at this!

# Contents

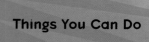

**Things You Can Do**

# For the Naked Housekeeper

# For the Naked Businessman

# For the Naked Handyman

# For the Naked Romantic

# Random Acts of Nakedness

# For the Naked Chef

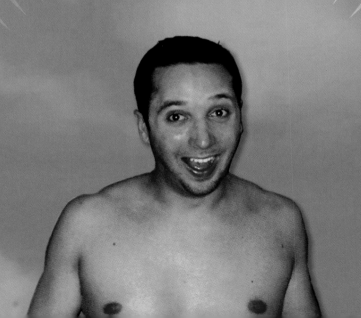

# Naked BBQ'ing

**A**n important thing to remember about throwing a good old-fashioned barbeque is to make sure you don't overcook your wieners. (You especially want to be careful when barbequing in the nude . . . be sure that ONLY your Oscar Mayer wieners end up on the grill!) If you're like Naked Guy and like to toast your buns, make certain you keep a close eye on them while they are browning. Buns can easily catch fire, and nobody likes a charred bun.

If you want a juicy, tender slab of meat, timing is everything. It is important to remember that there may be only a minute or two between a moist pork chop and a dry, leathery one. You can check for doneness by using an instant-read thermometer. Insert the thermometer into the thickest part of the meat to measure the internal temperature. If you don't have a thermometer, you can do it the old-fashioned way . . . just slice open your meat to see if it's cooked to your liking!

# Naked Marinara Sauce

**I**f you're a fan of Italian cooking, having a great marinara sauce recipe is a must. The following is a simple, yet delightful recipe that can be used with any classic pasta dish:

1/4 cup of olive oil

1 35-ounce can of imported plump and juicy italian tomatoes

1 cup water

4 cloves of garlic

1/2 teaspoon of oregano

4 basil leaves, chopped

Salt and pepper to taste

Place garlic and olive oil in saucepan. On medium heat cook until garlic is soft and browned. Crush the tomatoes and add their juices. Add 1 cup water to tomatoes and then add the basil, oregano, salt, and pepper. Bring ingredients to a boil, then lower to a simmer and cook until sauce is thickened (approx. 25 minutes). Pour over your favorite pasta and serve with crisp, hot garlic bread!

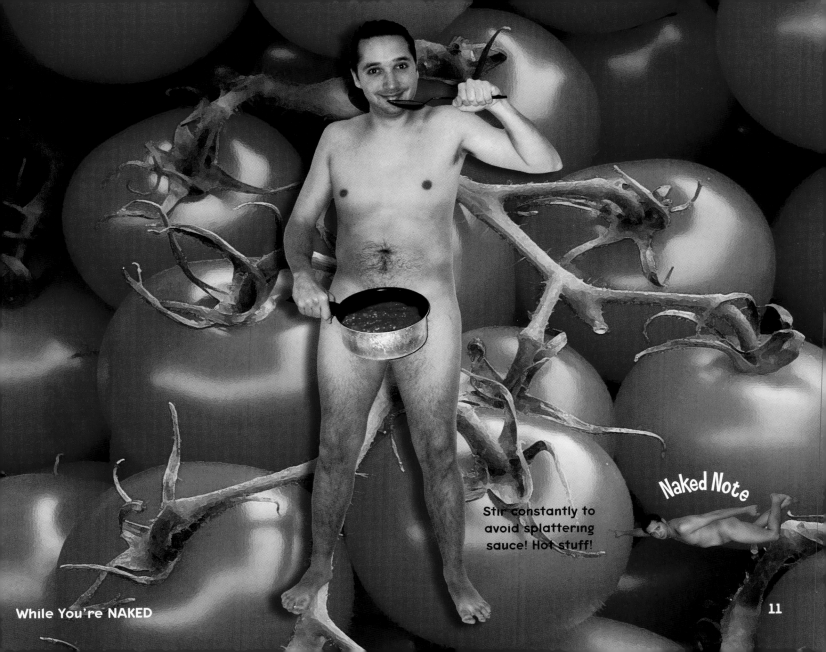

# Naked Couscous

Couscous, a staple of Middle Eastern cuisine, and Naked Guy's favorite dish, is a rice-like dish with a nutty taste that is a nice accompaniment to most meals. Instead of preparing rice or potatoes with your next dinner, switch it up by preparing couscous. Here's Naked Guy's favorite couscous recipe:

1 tablespoon canola oil
2 tablespoons chopped flat-leaf parsley
$1^{1}/_{2}$ cups chicken broth or water
1 cup plain couscous
$1/_{2}$ cup chopped scallions
Salt and freshly ground black pepper

In a medium saucepan, combine the oil and chicken broth or water, and bring to a simmer. Stir in the scallions and couscous and cover pan. Remove pan from the heat and let stand for five minutes.

When the couscous has absorbed all the liquid, fluff it with a fork, add parsley, salt, and pepper. Serve warm with your favorite piece of meat. Enjoy!

**While You're NAKED**

# Naked Pizza Making

**B**uon Giorno! Occasionally, it's fun to put away the take-out menus and make your own pizza! To get started you will need a simple pizza dough recipe:

3 1/2 cups flour
2 tablespoons honey
1 cup warm water
2 tablespoons yeast
1/2 teaspoon salt

Combine dough ingredients and get ready for the most pleasurable step in the pizza making process—kneading! Massage that big ball of dough with your hands. To avoid sticking, lube it up with olive oil! Be imaginative: use other body parts that may help in the kneading process. Rub your dough every which way until it begins to firm. Within minutes, you'll be able to stretch and shape your dough into the delicious foundation of your pizza.

After all that massaging, we're sure you've worked up quite an appetite! Adorn your dough with your favorite sauce (we recommend Naked Guy's Marinara sauce . . . delicious! see pg. 10). Sprinkle the top with liberal amounts of freshly grated mozzarella and cheddar cheese. Do you like a nice piece of meat? Try adding pieces of a big, juicy sausage. Bake at 450° for 18-24 minutes (ovens will vary), and when it's ready, *Mangia!*

PIZZA

Naked Note

Cheese graters are sharp . . .
proceed with caution!

15

# Naked Baking

Years ago, baking was a daily pastime. Sadly, the days of coming home to freshly baked cookies and homemade apple pies are quickly disappearing. Today, people are reluctant to beat it . . . . the batter, that is! Bring back the joy of baking by whipping up some cookies for your loved ones. The following is a tasty peanut butter cookie recipe:

$^1/_2$ cup butter

$^1/_2$ cup peanut butter

$^1/_2$ cup sugar

$^1/_2$ cup brown sugar

1 beaten egg

$1^1/_4$ cups flour

$^3/_4$ teaspoon baking soda

$^1/_4$ teaspoon salt

$^1/_2$ teaspoon vanilla

First mix the butter, peanut butter, and sugar together and cream well. (Warning: Don't get creative because you're naked. Search high and low for that missing wooden spoon . . . it's the ONLY thing you should stir your batter with!) Add beaten egg into the mixture. Sift flour once and add dry ingredients. Mix all wet and dry ingredients together and chill well. Now, using your hands, roll your dough into balls about the size of a walnut and dip them in sugar. Place your dipped balls onto a greased sheet and flatten with a fork. Bake at 375° for 10–12 minutes.

For the

Naked Sports Enthusiast

# Naked Nerf Basketball

**M**om always said, "Don't play ball in the house." But thanks to Nerf's plush, foam basketball, you can play with your balls anywhere you want! Playing naked basketball can help you work on your form . . . all of it! Without the restrictions of a polyester uniform, it's easier to get it up—the ball that is! Practice your jump shot, free throws, and rebounding. Work on your pivots and try some vertical leap exercises to heighten your jump for those three-point shots. Practice hard and practice often! You'll want to be nimble and quick so you can drive it to the hole in your next big game.

This stimulating activity is a great way to build endurance and is sure to be a slam dunk!

While You're NAKED

# Naked Cleaning Your Hunting Gun

**T**here is nothing quite as manly as a man with a hunting gun. To really get your testosterone flowing, get your hunting gun out of your rifle case, even if you don't have a hunting trip planned. Simply holding that gun in your hands will make you feel like a REAL man. Pause for a moment and think to yourself, "I can kill a furry woodland creature with this here gun. When I go huntin', I'll bring me home some nice venison."

Visualize your next big kill. Feel that macho blood flow through your body as you dream about firing at a fawn blissfully snacking on some grass in the rolling meadow.

Now, with a soft, dry cloth, shine up that gun of yours. You'll be glad you did when you're able to hang that deer head on the wall after your next hunting excursion.

HUNTIN'S IN
MY
BLOOD

While You're NAKED

# Naked Super Bowl Party

**W**ant to do something super? Naked Guy likes to host a Super Bowl party and invite his fellow football enthusiasts! Set the mood by hanging a banner to support your favorite team. You'll want to make sure your television is in a prime viewing location and that there is comfortable seating available for everyone.

As soon as guests arrive, offer up a cooler full of cold ones, then bring on the food! Be sure to get the extra points by serving creative and delicious hors d'oeuvres. Making your favorite finger foods will prevent you from getting stuck in the kitchen all night and missing out on the big plays. Present your party nuts, breadsticks, and cheese balls on a platter and accompany them with a variety of dips. Once your guests have feasted on the appetizing treats you've served, you can sit back, relax, and watch the big game. By hosting a Super Bowl party, you'll be sure to score a touchdown!

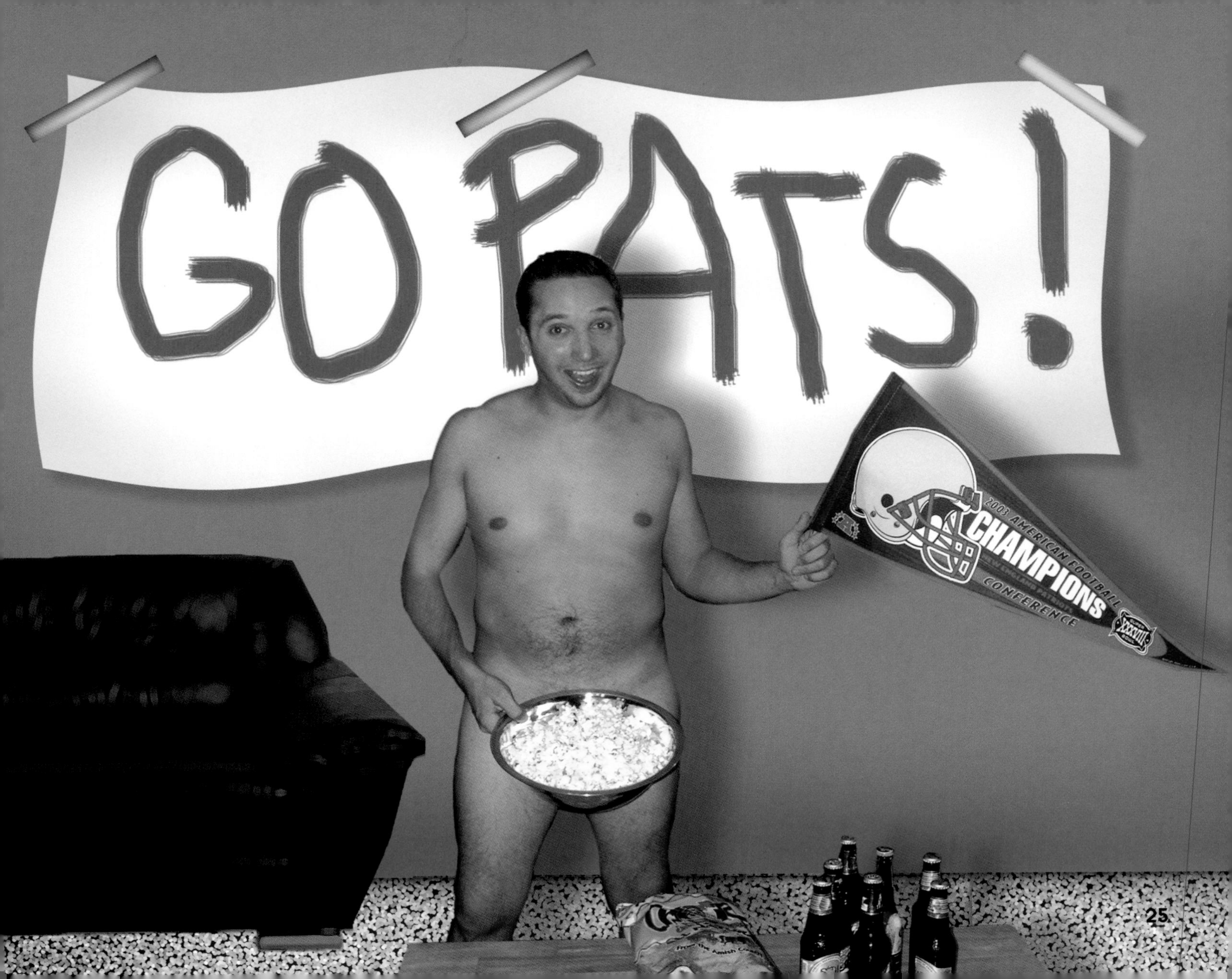
GO PATS!
2003 AMERICAN FOOTBALL
CHAMPIONS
CONFERENCE

# Naked Practicing Your Golf Swing

**I**f you are interested in climbing the corporate ladder, you may want to invite your boss to a round of golf at your next corporate outing. If you are feeling a little out of practice, fear not—you can work on your putt in the comfort of your own living room to avoid embarrassing yourself in front of the big guy. If you're not currently able to shoot a hole in one, you'll need to work on your short stroke. Select the proper club and make sure you adjust to the most comfortable grip on your driver's shaft. Pick your wedge and practice short, swift shots to the hole. Try a smooth putt . . . visualize, recognize, and execute! If you really want to make a good impression, make sure your wood is polished and your balls are washed before the big game (no one likes to play with dirty balls).

By looking like a pro on the golf course, your boss will consider you a pro on the job. You'll be sure to start climbing that corporate ladder in no time!

While You're NAKED

# Naked Texas Hold 'em

**N**aked Texas Hold'em is an updated style of the classic game of poker . . . with a few twists!

In this popular version, many of the rules are different but the object of the game is still the same: You want to have the best five-card poker hand!

Naked Guy enjoys playing Hold'em in the nude; the ecstasy of winning is more keenly felt. But be careful gentlemen—don't let your excitement show, or your opponents will clearly see that you have a good hand!

Bluffing is the ultimate deception in the game of Hold'em because it leaves fellow players believing you have a better hand than you really do. Men are particularly good at this as they often bluff about many things in their lives . . . like, say, their shoe size . . .

**Naked Note**

Naked Texas Hold'em may look and feel like you're playing (and losing) a game of strip poker, but remember to play by Hold'em rules!

For the

Naked Man of Leisure

# Naked Meditation

**I**f you've had a rough day dealing with unruly people, try meditation . . . in the nude! Naked Meditation is an incredible method you can use to release your negative energy. When you are naked, you are uninhibited, unrestricted, and free to focus on YOU.

Try stripping down and sitting down!

This mental exercise will help produce spiritual and emotional states like you've never experienced before. It is an easy way to detoxify yourself to the core.

Focus on your breathing. Try enunciating the "O" in "Ohmmmmmmm." Use your oral cavity, round your lips, and relax your jaw. By incorporating naked meditation into your everyday life, you'll be able to immunize yourself from whining children, a cranky spouse, and even that know-it-all mother-in-law!

# Ohmmm

# Naked Watching TV

**D**on't spend time fighting over the remote control! Show your "Bosom Buddies" "Who's the Boss" by taking control and tuning into your favorite re-runs! Maybe not everyone in your "Family Ties" enjoys TV hits from the '80s, but that's okay . . . "Diff'rent Strokes" for different folks! It's one of the "Facts of Life" that not everyone in your family will be in agreement all of the time.

Even if you were born with a "Silver Spoon" in your mouth, most people can appreciate the comedy of the 1980s! It'd be a "Small Wonder" if they didn't! Despite all the "Growing Pains" you may have experienced during "The Wonder Years," just think of all of the things you've learned from your favorite TV shows; you've learned not to talk to "Perfect Strangers" and not to do anything that might wind you up in "Night Court." But the most important lesson these shows taught you is to always try to be the "Greatest American Hero" you can be!

While You're NAKED

# Naked Knitting

**D**o you get a warm fuzzy feeling thinking about the afghan Grandma knit for you when you were young? One of your fondest childhood memories may be of cuddling up with one of her blankets and sipping hot cocoa beside a warm fire. Your memories don't have to be just memories. Make knitting blankets and other wonderful creations a thing of the present!

You'll be amazed at all the wonderful things you can create with two knitting needles and a ball of yarn! You could make a Christmas sweater for Mom, some mittens for the kids, a scarf for Dad, and even some potholders for Aunt Mildred. There are hundreds of possibilities!

Not only is knitting a great way to produce homemade gifts, but it is also an extremely relaxing hobby. You can release your mind while your fingers do the magic. Knit while you watch TV or create away while waiting to renew your license at the DMV. Knitting is no longer just a hobby for Grandma, but a stress-relieving hobby for all ages.

## Naked Note

Beware of becoming tangled in your yarn. Safely tuck away hair and other protruding body parts.

# Naked Reading

Those of you who have indulged in reading a smutty romance novel know the true pleasure these books can bring. Despite the fact that novels featuring Fabio on the cover are entertaining to any reader, men in particular may be embarrassed to openly reveal their love of such material.

Fear not, romance-novel-loving gents, there is a way around the embarrassment! Simply disguise that love story with something a bit more manly. Hide the novel inside of a do-it-yourself magazine or the sports section of the newspaper . . . this will conceal your passion for reading about the lust taking place on a far-off desert island. With your new macho novel disguise, you can freely follow Fabio through all of his romantic adventures!

While You're NAKED

# Naked Video-Gaming

Gone are the days of PacMan and Donkey Kong. The video games of today encompass action, adventure, fighting, racing, and intense competition! In order to succeed, you need to finish off your opponent quickly with rapid finger movements and a firm grasp on your controller. (Playing with a joystick is a definite thing of the past!)

With lifelike visuals and realistic sound effects, you may actually believe that you are the quarterback in a Monday Night Football game. Or, perhaps, you are on a mountaintop, slaying a dragon to save a princess. You may even be a rock star in your own band, on stage at your favorite venue! Regardless of what style of games you enjoy, you'll find that the games of today are a bit more complex and adventurous than your old favorites! Although times have changed, children of all ages can still come together to enjoy this pastime.

Naked Note

While engaging in some friendly competition, try sporting a man-eating grin . . . this will intimidate your competitor.

**While You're NAKED**

# Naked Intoxication

**A**fter a long, rough week at the office, there's nothing like cracking open a nice cold beer. Immediately you feel your tension and stress fade away. In fact, you feel so good, you decide to have another . . . what's the harm in one more, right? Before you know it, you are three or four beers deep and you haven't eaten since lunch. Suddenly that stale bag of tortilla chips and a three-day-old donut seem like the perfect dinner.

After you've enjoyed your wholesome meal, you find yourself looking for something fun and entertaining to do. We have just the game for you . . . Beer Goggle Stud! This is Naked Guy's favorite game to play when he is naked and intoxicated! To play, make your way to the bathroom mirror. Take a close look at yourself . . . after all of the alcoholic beverages you've consumed, you'll find that the man staring back at you is quite the hot stud. Now flex and convince yourself you're the sexiest man alive. This game of make-believe will keep you entertained for so long, you may need a nap!

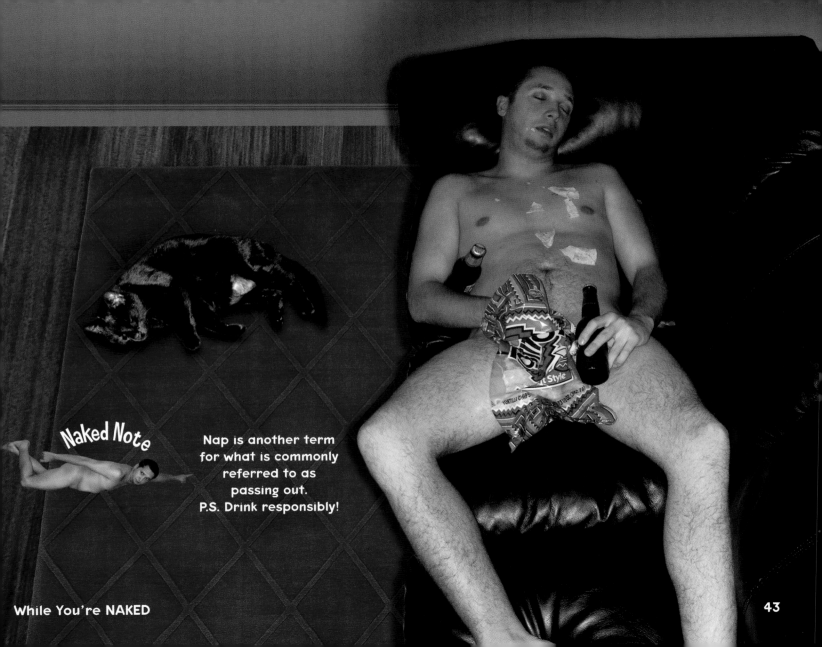

Naked Note

Nap is another term
for what is commonly
referred to as
passing out.
P.S. Drink responsibly!

For the
Naked Fitness Guru

# Naked Pilates

**R**esearch study after research study emphasizes the critical role that exercise plays in maintaining a healthy lifestyle. Taking care of your body is a necessity, but keeping the tummy toned and those buttocks tight isn't always easy. Pilates may be your answer to tightening up those areas that shouldn't be jiggling!

Pilates is a method of exercise and physical movement designed to stretch, strengthen, and balance the body. By holding slightly awkward positions and using specific breathing patterns, Pilates will help get muscles that you never knew you had into shape.

To enjoy Pilates in the comfort of your own home, you will need to purchase a Pilates video at your local video or health and fitness store. For comfort and control, purchase a yoga mat to aid in your routine. Pilates is sure to offer you the toning and tightening your body needs to make you feel confident in your favorite pair of jeans!

# Naked Jazzercise

**J**azzercise is a timeless workout experience like no other. This fitness routine includes jazz squares, jazz hands, lunges, and more! To accompany these moves, it is important to remember that the most significant element of a good jazzercise workout is the music. Please do not attempt to jazzercise without music that makes you want to shake your groove thing; disco is highly recommended.

As the upbeat music begins, use caution before diving right into the highly intense portion of your routine: you must warm up first. Find the beat of the music by tapping your toes. Then add finger snapping to your toe tapping and work your way up to incorporating miniature kicks. After you've worked up a small sweat, it's time to stretch so you can loosen your tight muscles. Try side lunges to loosen your groin area and toe touches to loosen your buttocks muscles. Continue to stretch until you feel nimble and agile.

Now you're ready to pump up the jam and really get your blood flowing. Let your body lose control! While jazzercising, not only will you enjoy an intense fitness routine, but you'll also discover a world of classic dance moves that previously were only learned in professional dance studios!

# Naked Trampolining

**N**aked trampolining is a high-impact aerobic workout of bouncing fun for every inch of your body. However, before you decide whether naked trampolining is for you, you must be properly informed. There are many different types of trampolines out there; you really need to do some serious research to find out which bounce is best for you.

If you are a beginner, you may want to consider starting off with a soft bounce trampoline. The soft bounce has a triple layer safety pad and comes with sturdy rubber footings. It is ideal for novice jumpers. There is also a smooth bounce trampoline which is perfect for intermediate-level jumpers. This trampoline offers a bit more spring, but ensures an even degree of bounce.

For those a bit more experienced (or daring!), you may want to consider the power bounce. This trampoline style offers the least amount of resistance and requires an advanced skill level.

Please keep in mind that naked trampolining is considerably different than trampolining with your clothes on. When you are naked, various limbs and body parts can rebound recklessly. Establishing a spring style that is comfortable for you is the key to successful bare bouncing!

# Naked Weightlifting

**W**eightlifting is an extremely important form of exercise when you're trying to transform your body into the cut, rippled, chiseled look you desire! Although you may not aspire to win The Strongest Man competition, it is still important to build and strengthen your muscles.

If you are new to the world of weightlifting, you should know that there are different ways to approach this form of exercise. Free weights are best for targeting specific muscle groups and will work areas like your biceps, chest, and triceps. Try using dumbbells to do curls and presses.

If you would prefer to work groups of muscles at a time, machines may be best for you. Machines provide resistance training and aid in toning.

Regardless of which route you choose, your body will reap the benefits of weight training. If you are a novice weightlifter, start off slowly. Naked Guy doesn't suggest trying to impress the ladies at the gym. Benching two times your body weight is not recommended and there's nothing more embarrassing than being pinned to the floor by the weights you couldn't lift!

### Naked Note

Gentlemen, please be advised that weightlifting does not strengthen your "love muscle."

# Naked Jumping Rope

Jumping rope is easy to learn and fun to do! There are a few key things you'll want to keep in mind when engaging in jumping rope:

1. Don't get tangled in your rope. This may sound ridiculous, but trust us, it can happen . . . especially when you are naked! A great way to avoid entanglement is to keep all hands and legs (among other protruding body parts) inside the swinging rope at all times!

2. Avoid rope burn. Due to the variety of jumps and movements you can learn with this exercise technique, the fast moving rope can become "whip-like" and slap you in the . . . . knee, causing a burn mark to occur. Ouch! Choose your moves wisely and only attempt those that don't exceed your skill level.

3. Unless you are an experienced jumper, DO NOT ATTEMPT Double Dutch under any circumstances. Double Dutch involves two jump ropes and can be extremely dangerous to newcomers of the sport.

Jumping rope is a classic and inexpensive way to jump-start your body into a fitter you.

While You're NAKED

For the

Naked Housekeeper

# Naked Trash Disposal

One major cause of relationship meltdown is the timeless argument about what should be considered trash. Since the beginning of time, women have been encouraging their men to throw away prized, grass-stained high school uniforms and practice shirts. Likewise, men have historically complained about the quantity of handbags and shoes many women have and want nothing more than to trash them all.

While we can't solve this dilemma for you, we do have some helpful advice:

Gentlemen—it's time to part with your sweat-stained past, just let go. Don't fool yourself by thinking you'll fit into your high school football jersey again some day.

Ladies—Men will never understand why there is a need to have all of those shoes and handbags. Find a good hiding place for them and if he finds your stash, deny, deny, deny!

We understand that the trash argument will continue to plague couples everywhere until the end of time. But please, try your best to limit the "trash talking" that often accompanies these arguments!

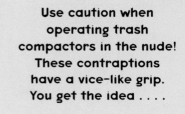

Use caution when
operating trash
compactors in the nude!
These contraptions
have a vice-like grip.
You get the idea . . . .

Naked Note

# Naked Vacuuming

**T**hink vacuuming is a drag? Well, unfortunately, if you want your house neat and clean, you're going to have to suck it up . . . literally! We have some advice on how to change your thoughts on this household chore.

From here forward, think of vacuuming as your audition to be the star of a steamy burlesque show. No longer are you vacuuming just to tidy up your floor, but you're also performing your sexiest moves for a panel of judges. Your vacuum is your stripper pole and your carpet is your stage, now show those judges what you've got!

Here are some of Naked Guy's moves that are sure to impress:

- Backwards vacuum between the legs: Start by standing spread eagle. Vacuum in a circle beginning in the front and circling around to your back. End the circle by pulling the vacuum through your legs.
- Vacuum spin to the floor: Dramatically pause while vacuuming. Hold the vacuum with your right hand and do a quick spin down to the floor releasing the vacuum half way through and grabbing it before it falls.
- Vacuum bucking bronco: Straddle and ride that vacuum like a wild horse!

Before you know it, your entire house will be vacuumed to perfection. More importantly, you will have invented some never-before-seen moves that you can pass on to your friends!

While You're NAKED

# Naked Pillow Fluffing

**D**oes your woman like her pillows fluffed?
There is so much more to making a bed than simply tucking in the sheets.

To ensure a good night's rest for your loved one, be sure to fluff her pillows every night before bedtime.

Whether she has soft, fluffy ones, or hard, supportive ones, paying attention to them every evening will help get her off to a comfortable, dreamy sleep.

Hold her pillows gently at the tips and shake.

If the pillow remains flattened, we recommend kneading it to restore its bounce.

Smooth her pillows with your hand and position them on the bed to your liking. By properly fluffing her pillows by day, you'll be certain to increase the amount of pillow talk you receive by night!

# Naked Ironing

**E**ven Naked Guy can't be naked all of the time; there are some daily activities that do require clothing. Though you'd rather attend your next sales meeting in the comfort of your own skin and nothing else, unfortunately the society we live in requires that you cover it up . . . all of it. if you want to make a good impression in the business world, you've got to "strike while the iron is hot" . . . literally!

As boring as ironing may be, it is the only way to look crisp and clean in your Sunday best. To combat the boredom, turn ironing into a game: challenge yourself to iron your clothes until they have fewer wrinkles than your Great Aunt Susan!

Let's face it, it's healthy and fun to laugh at the wrinkles and creases in your body, but it is not okay to take the wrinkles and creases in your clothing lightly!

While You're NAKED

# Naked Dusting

**D**ust can settle into the most unruly of places. Are you tired of wrestling with your cracks and crevices? To get the job done thoroughly, you need to work with suitable supplies. First things first: depending on how dusty your home is, you may want to consider wearing a filter mask. Obviously that will be the only thing you'll wear!

You'll also need the proper duster. Naked Guy recommends purchasing a feather duster; they're inexpensive and often able to get to those hard to reach places. We think feather dusters are the best in the in"dust"ry!

Next, you'll want to have a first-rate brand of furniture polish. The goal here is to remove the dust, not just brush it away. The right polish will help keep dust from resurfacing too quickly. Lastly, use a disinfecting spray. This will help remove any bacteria that may still be hovering over your living room.

By following these easy guidelines, you can create a dust-free environment for the whole family to enjoy!

For the Naked Businessman

# Naked Filing

**D**o you often find yourself searching for missing bills that need to be paid or forms that need to be faxed? All of this wasted time and frustration can be avoided with the simple purchase of a filing cabinet.

By using a filing system, you'll have accurate up-to-date records of your bills and bank statements. Next time the cable company phones to tell you you're past due, you can "stick it to the man" by supplying them with a copy of your cashed check! Consider for a moment how great it will be to be able to provide proof to the IRS that you did not cheat them and do not owe thousands of dollars in back taxes and penalties! Naked or not, everyone knows you "don't mess with the IRS." By being organized and consistent with your records, you can save your bare assets.

Things You Can Do

# Naked Conference Calling

**N**aked Guy understands that it is imperative for a good businessman to keep the appearance of having his emotions under control at all times. The rule of thumb for successful communication in any business environment is to always stay calm, cool, collected . . . and clothed!

However, while making business calls in the comfort of your own home office, your voice is the only thing that needs to remain calm. In addition, you can feel free to take it all off and strip down to the bare necessities.

While you speak ever-so-pleasantly to your annoying client or business partner over the phone, feel free to throw something across the room or give him/her the finger right through the receiver to alleviate stress. If that doesn't seem to work, you can jump up and down and hold your breath while all the blood rushes to your neck and face. . . see, throwing a silent temper tantrum while on a conference call is easy!

The best part about naked conference calling is that no one you work with will ever know about your bad behavior. Just make sure it isn't a video conference call, especially if you're calling in the buff!

While You're NAKED

# Naked Tax Evasion

**I**f you are a corrupt business owner and are planning to fudge the numbers or attempt to evade your tax payments, hopefully you learned a thing or two from our friends at Enron: SHRED, SHRED, SHRED! In case of an investigation, shredding important documents is a surefire way to throw off the Feds. Remember, as the depth of your deception grows, you will need to become an expert at lying about your profit, concealing your debts, and laundering your money. Hiding your files is just not enough when it comes to fooling the government. You must destroy all evidence!

However, it is important to remember that shredding isn't always a foolproof method. If the IRS comes knocking on your door with hundreds of rolls of scotch tape and finds your bags of shredded incriminating evidence, you could be in major trouble! To sleep soundly at night, you may want to add burning those paper shreds into your scheme.

# Naked Budgeting

**S**ometimes it may feel like your hard-earned money is spent faster than you can make it. With so many monthly bills to pay, it's hard to stay on top of things. That's exactly why establishing a household budget is important. A budget will allow you to keep an eye on those high-interest credit cards and help you pay them off sooner. It will also allow you to pay your bills on time, and help you set aside some money into a savings account.

This savings, in turn, will permit you to make that large purchase you've been wanting! Whether it's a new home, a new car, a Swedish penis enlarger, whatever . . . you'll be able to acquire your much desired item sooner! However, please be advised that it's important to consult with your significant other before committing to an expensive purchase. Be sure it's an item you'll both reap the benefits of!

# Naked Computing

**I**n a world run by technology, your computer can be the key to running a successful business. Quicker access to information, ease of communication via e-mail, and online commerce are just a few elements that a computer can add to your bottom line.

Your hard drive can be used to store important information, and using your floppy is a great way to store files that may need to be shared.

We recommend, if you are planning to work naked from home on a regular basis, that you invest in a laptop, which will allow you to work from virtually anywhere in the house. Naked Guy finds it stimulating to compute from his lap . . . keeping his lower extremities warm in those cold winter months!

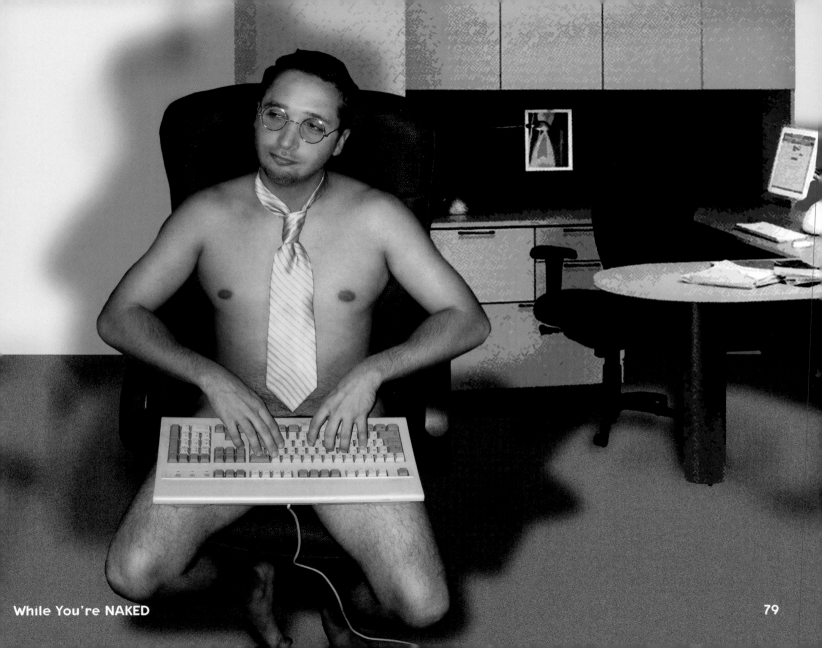

# For the
# Naked Handyman

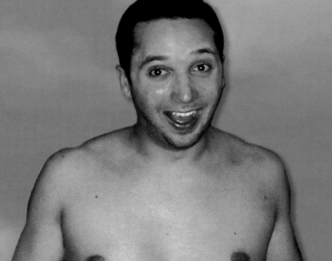

# Naked Crown Molding Installation

**A**re you a do-it-yourselfer? You can be! Have you always dreamed of crown molding to complete the look of your bedroom or dining room? Now you can install it all on your own! By making a trip to your local hardware store, you can ask questions, buy the right tools, and learn how to create that finished look you've always wanted.

Before embarking on this adventure, Naked Guy has a few tips: Always wear safety goggles, make sure you begin with all the needed equipment and supplies, and watch as many home improvement shows as you can! To learn more about installation, safety, and proper measurements, you can also refer to handyman websites. In no time at all you'll achieve that finished look in your home that you've been craving.

# Naked Picture Hanging

One way to take your home from drab to fab is by hanging paintings or other artwork on your empty walls. Not only can hanging art be a décor enhancer, but it can also help cover up blemishes on your walls. Instead of running out to your local hardware store for spackle to fill that hole you punched, cover it with framed art. Did your wife throw a dish at you and miss? Cover that unsightly dent with a Picasso reprint.

Please be advised to hang your artwork with care. For the best results, Naked Guy uses the following tools: a tape measure, a hammer, a level, a pencil, and a stud finder (please do not point the stud finder at yourself and say you "found the stud." It's an old joke and it isn't very funny). Measure the exact height at which you wish to hang your picture. Draw a light line with your pencil to indicate where to place the nails. Hammer your nails at a slight angle and simply hang your artwork. Test your work with a level and adjust as needed. Picture hanging can be a colorful experience for you and your home!

# Naked Plumbing

**I**f you are comfortable with the basics of plumbing, you're likely to save yourself a lot of time and headaches. If you're not familiar with the basic techniques, it's time to learn. A quick way to learn is to take apart the piping under your kitchen sink. Pay careful attention to how the pipes connect—you're going to need to know this when it's time to put it back together. If your faucet happens to be leaky, now is a good time to cock it.

If there is only one reason to learn about plumbing it is this: wedding ring retrieval! If you are married, or planning to get married one day, chances are your spouse will throw his or her ring down the drain at some point. Even if you are glad the relationship is over, you're going to want that ring back so you can sell it to your local pawn shop. And guys, if the relationship isn't over and her actions were simply high drama, the pressure will be on you to get that ring back! The sooner you learn proper plumbing techniques, the better . . . it could save you big $$$$.

While You're NAKED

# Naked Toilet Plunging

**Y**ou've spent an entire Saturday evening stuffing your face with your favorite spicy Indian dish. As you ate, you knew what was in store for you the next morning, but at the time you didn't care. You wake up Sunday with those familiar stomach cramps and run for the bathroom.

After 20 minutes of agony, it takes almost an entire roll of toilet paper to clean up. You flush . . . not all of it goes down . . . you flush again . . . no response. You've done it again—you've clogged the toilet! Time for some good, old-fashioned toilet plunging.

Follow Naked Guy's instructions below for the most effective plunging technique (as he's had a lot of practice at this!):

**Step One:** Get out your plunger and assume a full lunge position next to the toilet.

**Step Two:** Place the rubber plunger in the bowl, making sure to cover the entire inner hole.

**Step Three:** Swiftly pump the plunger using all of the elbow grease you have left in you (you may be tired after what it took to create this mess).

**Step Four:** As you feel suction in the bowl, attempt to flush. If it doesn't flush, repeat step three.

Naked Note

Wear rubber gloves . . .
in fact, wear a rubber
apron if that makes you
feel better about
the situation!

# Naked Woodworking

**W**oodworking is tricky business. Sure, those home improvement shows make it look easy, but it is a very precise and intricate trade. However, if you're willing to take on the challenge, you'll be amazed at what you can accomplish. From fixing the post on your staircase, to building an armoire for your bedroom, there are literally thousands of things you can create.

Your interests may also extend to the exterior of your home. Perhaps you'd like to build a tree house for the kids. Or maybe you would like to put up a fence to give your yard a bit more privacy. (If you plan to spend time outdoors while you're naked, you may seriously want to consider this!) Regardless of which home improvement ideas sound good to you, be sure to educate yourself and work with the proper materials and safety gear. You'll be sure to increase the value of your home in no time!

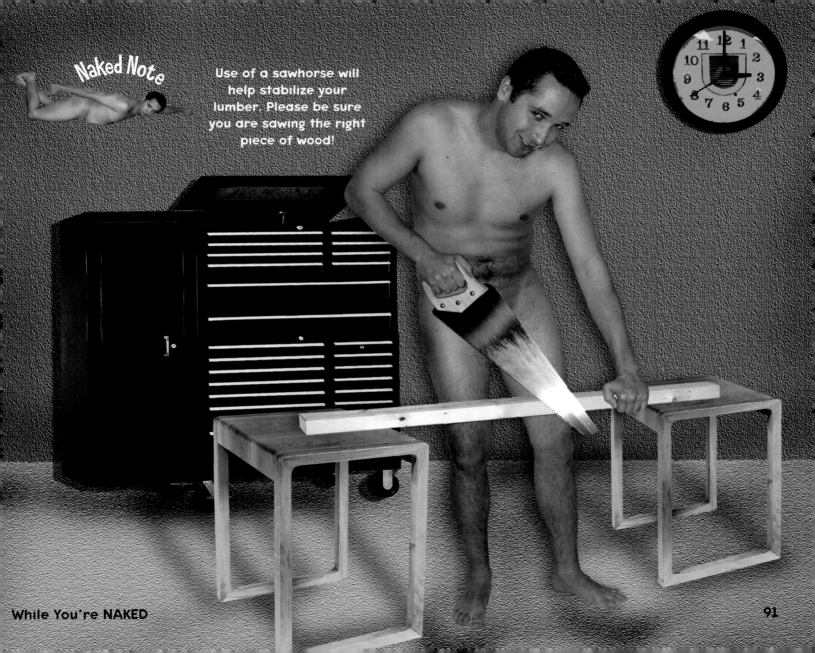

# For the Naked Romantic

# Naked Flower Arranging

Oh no, you've done it again, you've upset your girlfriend or wife. You've given her the same sad sob story of "I won't do it again" too many times. You're going to have to do something big to make it up to her this time; a rinky-dink daisy bouquet from the grocery store isn't going to cut it. To win her over, you have to create an extravagant floral arrangement all on your own. Not only will you be giving her gorgeous flowers, but you'll also be putting in a lot of obvious effort. Remember guys, it's the effort that counts the most!

Here's a list of some statement-making flowers you can incorporate to send the right message when creating your perfect arrangement: violets, forget-me-nots, pansies, roses, tulips, daisies, and irises. An arrangement containing any combination of these will say anything from, "i am innocent," to "i am passionate," to "i love you."

There are no rules for assembly, just follow your heart. To score more points, write a poem or bake some cookies to accompany the arrangement. She won't be able to stay mad at you when she sees all the trouble you've gone through.

# Naked Aromatic Candle Lighting

In order to properly seduce your loved one, you must appeal to all five senses. The sense of smell is commonly overlooked when it comes to evoking feelings of romance. Using scented candles in a romantic setting adds more pleasure to the mix by stimulating the olfactory nerves. Plus, gazing at a flame can be a mesmerizing experience that relaxes both the eyes and the mind.

Let's face it, if your home smells of trash and pet odor, the romance will be killed instantly! By taking the time to create a deliciously scented environment, you are showing your loved one that you pay attention to detail. Naked Guy suggests that if your honey has a love for the beach, light an ocean-scented candle. If his or her fondness is for chocolate, light a chocolate-mousse-scented candle to fill the room. Stimulating your lover's sense of smell will surely leave him or her craving for more!

**Naked Note**

Lighting matches off
your body only works
in the movies.

# Naked Sexy Pose Practicing

**N**othing says "come hither" better than sultry, seductive eyes. You can express a lot of emotion with those babies . . . so take advantage. By narrowing your eyes at the corners and pursing your lips, you're saying, "Don't you want me?" By keeping your eyes in that same narrowed position and curving your lips upward in a mischievous smile, you're saying, "You know I want you."

To properly seduce someone, you've got to have these looks down pat . . . you wouldn't want the object of your seduction to think you have something in your eye.

Practice posing in the mirror. Imagine you are the object of your own affection (which in many cases, may not be too much of a stretch!). See if you can thrill yourself! Use your body language to entice your lover. A suggestive pose cries out, "I'm ready for you!"

Naked Note

Use caution when using seductive poses. You may get more than what you bargained for . . . .

While You're NAKED

# Naked Proposal Practicing

Cupid has drawn back his bow and shot you clear in the heart with his arrow! You know you've found the love of your life and now it's time to pop the big question. Think "perfect proposal practicing" is a tongue twister? Just wait until the time comes to actually propose for real! Don't let your nervousness and excitability get in the way of those perfect words you wish to utter while popping the question. While you are kneeling in front of her, you certainly wouldn't want the words, "Will you marry me?" to come out sounding like "You have hairy knees." While you tell her "I can't wait to grow old with you," you don't want her to accidentally hear "You smell like a dirty old shoe." You only have one shot at reciting the perfect speech.

Naked Guy knows that rehearsal is the key to a successful proposal. Grab a ring box and get down on one knee in front of a mirror. Practice looking into her eyes and telling her how much she means to you. If you can convince yourself you're worth marrying, you may just have a shot at hearing a "Yes!" to your question. Good luck!

# Random Acts of Nakedness

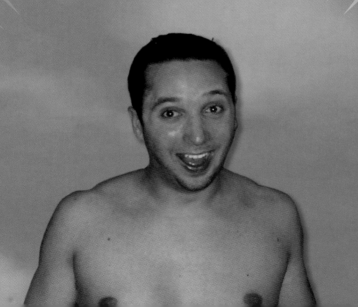

# Naked Magic Tricks

**N**ow you see it, now you don't! Like playing tricks? With a simple deck of cards, a handkerchief, a rubber ball, a coin, and a white rabbit, you can perform easy, crowd-pleasing tricks right in the comfort of your own home! Pull a rabbit out of your hat, hide a coin behind someone's ear, set a newspaper on fire and extinguish the flame without a single drop of water. You can even make your assistant magician disappear! We don't, however, feel novice magicians should attempt to saw assistants in half! This is clearly a trick for professionals!

By purchasing a few magic trick kits and reading up on your favorite magician, you'll be sure to be the best magic act in town . . . and that's not smoke and mirrors!

# Naked Record Collecting

**S**tarting a collection is a great way to express your passion for something you love. Whether it's baseball cards, stamps, old coins, or even Pez dispensers, displaying your collectables is the best way to showcase your love and appreciation for them. Naked Guy enjoys record collecting. He feels that having an eclectic record collection says a lot about him as a person. if record collecting may be something you'd enjoy, make the most of your collection by representing every genre of music and every style of artist out there. That way, when friends come over you'll be sure to have something for everyone!

# Naked Take-Out

**A**fter a long hard day, the last thing you want to do is cook an entire dinner. What to do? Follow Naked Guy's lead and call your local pizza/sub shop and order in! In roughly 30 minutes, you can have a hot, ready-to-eat meal arrive at your doorstep! No fuss, no mess, no stress! All you have to do is set up your TV tray and answer the front door—the rest is taken care of!

In case your buffalo wings arrive with a pathetic portion of blue cheese dressing, try to have some extra on hand . . . that way you'll never be disappointed. We also recommend adding hot sauce, soy sauce, duck sauce, and a variety of salad dressings to your grocery list. You'll never be short on condiments for your take-out orders and you'll always be satisfied!

Naked Note

Many delivery drivers may not be expecting to meet a naked customer at the front door—you may want to notify them in advance or wrap yourself in a blanket!

# Naked Shadow Puppeteering

Shadow puppeteering is a commonly overlooked, yet innovative, way to get in touch with your artistic side. This art form is an expressive approach to exploring the depths of your inner-self and an open door to the core of your creativity.

Step One: Start by holding your hands out in front of you. Explore the distinctive hand gestures and flowing movements you can craft.

Step Two: Now that you have observed the full potential of your very own hands, you are ready to begin creating your own masterpiece! Stand between an empty wall and a bright light. Become one with your shadow.

Step Three: Now, really start to get into character. Don't be afraid to incorporate facial expressions with your hand gestures. Use your body language to bring out the true animation you have from within.

Step Four: Results! Admire your creation and revel in your artistic fire!

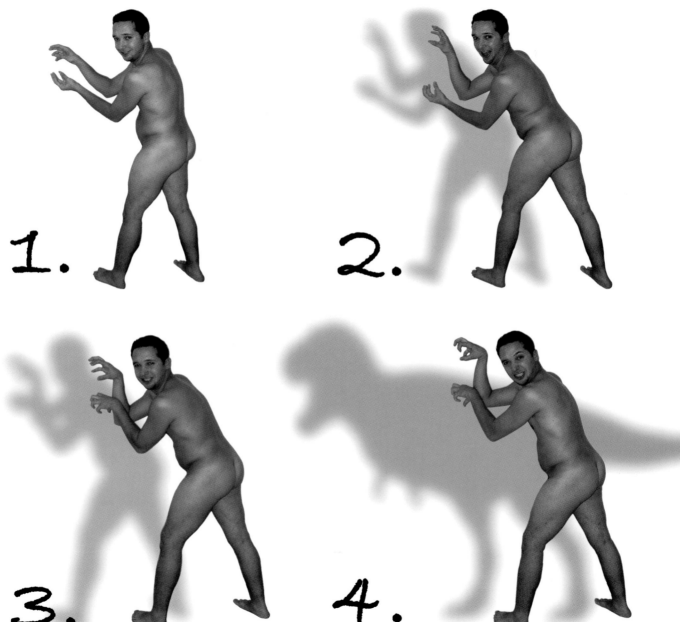

# Books Available from Santa Monica Press

www.santamonicapress.com • 1-800-784-9553

**American Hydrant**
by Sean Crane
176 pages  $24.95

**Atomic Wedgies, Wet Willies &**
**Other Acts of Roguery**
by Greg Tananbaum and Dan Martin
128 pages  $11.95

**The Bad Driver's Handbook**
*Hundreds of Simple Maneuvers to*
*Frustrate, Annoy, and Endanger Those*
*Around You*
by Zack Arnstein and Larry Arnstein
192 pages  $12.95

**The Butt Hello**
*and other ways my cats drive me crazy*
by Ted Meyer
96 pages  $9.95

**Calculated Risk**
*The Extraordinary Life of Jimmy Doolittle*
by Jonna Doolittle Hoppes
360 pages  $24.95

**Can a Dead Man Strike Out?**
*Offbeat Baseball Questions*
*and Their Improbable Answers*
by Mark S. Halfon
192 pages  $11.95

**Captured!**
*Inside the World of Celebrity Trials*
by Mona Shafer Edwards
Text by Jody Handley
184 pages  $24.95

**Creepy Crawls**
*A Horror Fiend's Travel Guide*
by Leon Marcelo
384 pages  $16.95

**Dogme Uncut**
*Lars von Trier, Thomas Vinterberg*
*and the Gang That Took on Hollywood*
by Jack Stevenson
312 pages  $16.95

**Elvis Presley Passed Here**
*Even More Locations of America's*
*Pop Culture Landmarks*
by Chris Epting
336 pages  $16.95

**Exotic Travel Destinations**
**for Families**
by Jennifer M. Nichols and Bill Nichols
360 pages  $16.95

**Footsteps in the Fog**
*Alfred Hitchcock's San Francisco*
by Jeff Kraft and Aaron Leventhal
240 pages  $24.95

**French for Le Snob**
*Adding Panache to Your*
*Everyday Conversations*
by Yvette Reche
400 pages  $16.95

**Haunted Hikes**
*Spine-Tingling Tales and Trails from*
*North America's National Parks*
by Andrea Lankford
372 pages  $16.95

**How to Speak Shakespeare**
by Cal Pritner and Louis Colaianni
144 pages  $16.95

**Jackson Pollock:**
**Memories Arrested in Space**
by Martin Gray
216 pages  $14.95

**James Dean Died Here**
*The Locations of America's*
*Pop Culture Landmarks*
by Chris Epting
312 pages  $16.95

**The Keystone Kid**
*Tales of Early Hollywood*
by Coy Watson, Jr.
312 pages  $24.95

**L.A. Noir**
*The City as Character*
by Alain Silver and James Ursini
176 pages  $19.95

**Loving Through Bars**
*Children with Parents in Prison*
by Cynthia Martone
216 pages  $21.95

**Marilyn Monroe Dyed Here**
*More Locations of America's*
*Pop Culture Landmarks*
by Chris Epting
312 pages  $16.95

**Movie Star Homes**
by Judy Artunian and Mike Oldham
312 pages  $16.95

**My So-Called Digital Life**
*2,000 Teenagers, 300 Cameras,*
*and 30 Days to Document Their World*
by Bob Pletka
176 pages  $24.95

**Offbeat Museums**
*The Collections and Curators of*
*America's Most Unusual Museums*
by Saul Rubin
240 pages  $19.95

**Opening Lines, Pinky Probes,**
**and L-Bombs**
*The Girls & Sports Dating and*
*Relationship Playbook*
by Justin Borus and Andrew Feinstein
144 pages  $14.95

**A Prayer for Burma**
by Kenneth Wong
216 pages  $14.95

**Quack!**
*Tales of Medical Fraud from the Museum*
*of Questionable Medical Devices*
by Bob McCoy
240 pages  $19.95

**Redneck Haiku**
*Double-Wide Edition*
by Mary K. Witte
240 pages  $11.95

**Route 66 Adventure Handbook**
*Expanded Third Edition*
by Drew Knowles
384 pages  $16.95

**The Ruby Slippers, Madonna's Bra,**
**and Einstein's Brain**
*The Locations of America's*
*Pop Culture Artifacts*
by Chris Epting
312 pages  $16.95

**School Sense: How to Help Your**
**Child Succeed in Elementary School**
by Tiffani Chin, Ph.D.
408 pages  $16.95

**Silent Echoes**
*Discovering Early Hollywood*
*Through the Films of Buster Keaton*
by John Bengtson
232 pages  $24.95

**Silent Traces**
*Discovering Early Hollywood*
*Through the Films of Charlie Chaplin*
by John Bengtson
304 pages  $24.95

**Things You Can Do**
**While You're Naked**
by Jaime Andrews and Jessica Doherty
112 pages  $12.95

**Tiki Road Trip**
*A Guide to Tiki Culture in*
*North America*
by James Teitelbaum
288 pages  $16.95